These People Mine portrays Mennonites as a people caught between tradition and a dream. Strong poetry and an extended parable sensitively bind together symbolic vignettes from the Mennonite past.

The author explores the beginnings of the Mennonite family of churches some 400 years ago, their migrations to America, the collision of Amish and Mennonite ideals with the twentieth century, and the growth of the church through missions.

Mennonites today are a people diverse in origin, in character, and in their particular contribution to the rest of mankind.

These People Mine originally premiered as a musical drama at Curitiba, Brazil, in July 1972. Photographs of contemporary Amish and Mennonites as well as from the drama production add interest to the book.

These People Mine

by Merle Good

 Herald Press, Scottdale, Pennsylvania

These People Mine

Copyright © 1973 by Good Enterprises Limited
Library of Congress Catalog Card Number: 73-6196
International Standard Book Number: 0-8361-1718-2
Printed in the United States
Book designed by Jan Gleysteen

to Phyllis

Other works by Merle Good

Book

Happy as the Grass Was Green

Dramas

Strangers at the Mill

Who Burned the Barn Down?

Sons Like Their Fathers

Yesterday, Today, and Forever

A Lot of Love

Preface

I must have been crazy. How else can I explain my acceptance of an invitation to write a drama for the Ninth Mennonite World Conference to be held in Curitiba, Brazil, during July, 1972? How in the world does one write a piece representing our people all over the globe, and at the same time seek to say something halfway fresh and meaningful about our varied lives?

I suppose it took a bit of faith to write *These People Mine*. I believed there was something to say, something to point to, something to probe. So, expecting the worst, yet knowing that God uses imperfect people like me all the time, I plunged into what seemed an impossible task.

From the beginning I was determined to write about ourselves and God's work among us in a way that permitted those unfamiliar with our way of life to see us for what we are: a pilgrim people, caught between a dream and a tradition, scattered to our various "promised land" settlements all over the earth, seeking a new day but fearing its light. I knew *These People Mine* would premiere at Mennonite World Conference in a basically friendly atmosphere; but I also knew it would be staged night after night at our

Festival in Lancaster, where "the world" could look at it from outside and say "That stinks!" (which being interpreted generally means "You stink!").

The theme I attempted to explore throughout *These People Mine* is one that has fascinated me for many years: Is the church homogeneous or heterogeneous? Does the true Christian community consist of people with common backgrounds, interests, and concepts? Or is the real church made up of people of unlike nationalities, symbols, and ideas who have their faith as their only likeness? The question can never be fully answered, perhaps, but at least some possible answers can be explored. Reunion hopes have always been part of the Mennonite answer.

This book is based on the drama script. Photos of the original cast accompany the text. The scenes have been transcribed into short stories. The lyrics of the songs are printed here as poetry. And a narrative unity has been added in the form of a symbolic parable.

Translation is planned for *These People Mine* into German, Spanish, and Portuguese. A North American tour of the drama is slated for summer, 1973, to be followed by a four-week run at the

Dutch Family Festival in Lancaster, Pennsylvania.

I wish to thank the dozens of friends and fellow-believers who helped this project come to pass. A word of appreciation goes to Cornelius J. Dyck for writing "An Introduction to the Mennonites and Amish" and to William Snyder for his introduction. And I say a special "thank you" to my wife and partner, Phyllis, to whom this book is dedicated, for her love, courage, and faith, and for her gift of being the other of my life.

Merle Good
Lancaster, Pennsylvania
New Year's Day, 1973

Introduction

The drama of the Anabaptist movement from its early birth pangs in Europe through the testing grounds in many countries is fascinating.

These People Mine relates how the simple faith of the early Anabaptists — later dubbed Mennonites — survived martyrdom, migration, war, and hunger to spearhead the establishment of freedom of faith and conscience in the western world.

The narrative is significant in the seventies because controversies are again arising regarding the relationship of church and state.

The insight and courage shown in this drama of the Anabaptists is needed today as we ponder the role of modern Christians as people of salt and light in society.

William T. Snyder, *Executive Secretary*
Mennonite Central Committee
Akron, Pennsylvania

Contents

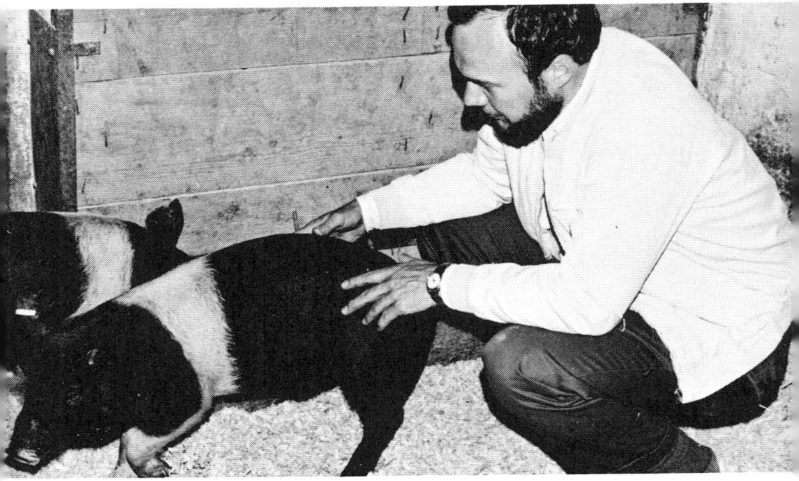

Mennonite Central Committee worker Coletta Lora Wiebe from Beatrice, Nebraska, teaches a class of Brazilian children the relationship between diet and energy.

David Gerber, Smithville, Ohio, Mennonite Central Committee director for Crete, with two Hampshire boars MCC sent to help improve agriculture on the island.

14

An Introduction to the Mennonites and Amish

THE STORY of the Mennonites and the Amish begins in the time of the Reformation in Europe in the sixteenth century, and continues some four hundred and fifty years to the present day.

From a few groups in Switzerland, Holland, and Germany their decendants have spread across the globe in all directions and are now found not only in North America, but also South America, Africa, Russia, Asia, and Australia. Yet they are still a small group of only one half million people, of whom one third are nonwhite.

In their religious beliefs Mennonites and Amish are more alike than different, but in their social and cultural ways they are different. The Amish are mostly farmers. Members of most Amish groups use horses instead of tractors and drive buggies instead of cars to keep from becoming too deeply involved in the things of the world which they fear might destroy their trust in God.

The Amish maintain their own schools wherever possible. They terminate formal education with the eighth grade, but church and home continue to instruct children in the Amish ways.

They wear beards and plain clothing, and are sometimes called "the plain people."

Culturally, most Mennonites differ not only from the Amish but also among themselves much as people of different cultures and traditions differ from each other. Some Mennonites wear beards, too, but like as not because it is popular today to do so. They believe deeply in education and are found as students and teachers at universities across the land in most of the major professions. Mennonites also have their own colleges and graduate seminaries, and some groups maintain their own high schools.

Many Mennonites are farmers, using the latest agricultural techniques. They are generally considered to be thrifty and hardworking. They are involved in the civic affairs of their communities as any citizen would be. A few hold political offices.

In recent years many people who have suffered disasters like tornadoes, hurricanes, or floods have met Mennonites and Amish for the first time who came to help in the clean-up process as Mennonite Disaster Service volunteers.

A New Birth Is Important

Mennonites received their name from Menno Simons (d. 1561), a Dutch Catholic priest who was one of the early leaders of the movement. They would rather have been known as *Brethren*, which is what they called themselves when they formed the first congregation in Switzerland

Despite their refusal to use modern machinery and electricity, the Amish achieve excellent production on well-kept farms. They fear that becoming involved in the world might destroy their trust in God.

in 1525, but their opponents kept referring to them as Mennonites.

They were also called *Anabaptists* (from the Latin word for rebaptism) because they baptized adult believers only, even if they had earlier been baptized as children. Why did they do this? Because they believed that baptism was a visible symbol of a mature decision to follow Christ and obey His commands.

An unknown Mennonite preacher said in 1527 in one of the earliest sermons discovered from that period: "Except we are born anew we cannot see the kingdom of God (John 3). There is no other birth, for whoever hears the Word of God and receives it into his heart, all which the Word teaches in his heart he is willing to do according to the will of God (1 Peter 4). If he does this, no longer doing the will of the world but the will of God, he is a true child of God; he is also truly born again."

In this they were all agreed. Another of their leaders, Pilgram Marpeck, a civil engineer in Augsburg, Germany, at that time wrote, "And this is the covenant in baptism, that we, through the knowledge of the Lord and Savior, Jesus Christ, put off and flee the filth of the world and bind ourselves with Christ to a new life."

Hans Denck, a teacher, wrote, "The conversion must take place from the roots of our existence. To Christ we should bring empty souls." And Menno Simons confirmed this conviction by writing two separate books about it. Sometimes he spoke of a new birth, sometimes of a spiritual resurrection, or a new creation, or

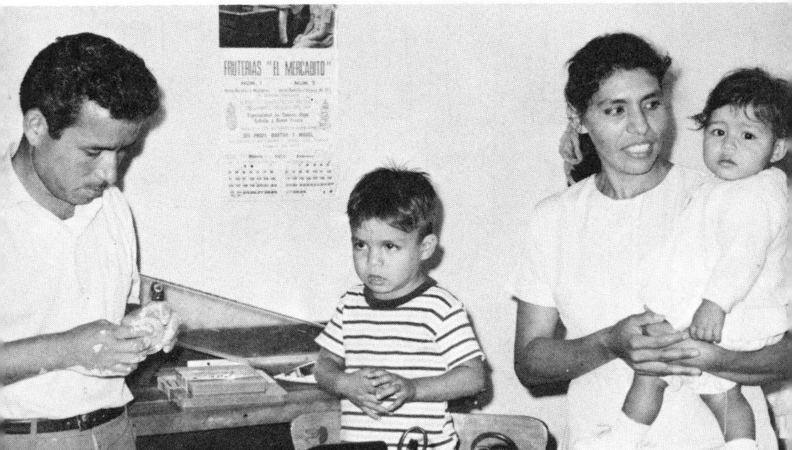

Jeremiah Ross, a Canadian Indian, pastors the Mennonite congregation at Cross Lake, Manitoba.

Alfonso Munoz Sanchez, pastor of the Mennonite church in Reynosa, Mexico, with his wife, Marta, and two of their four children.

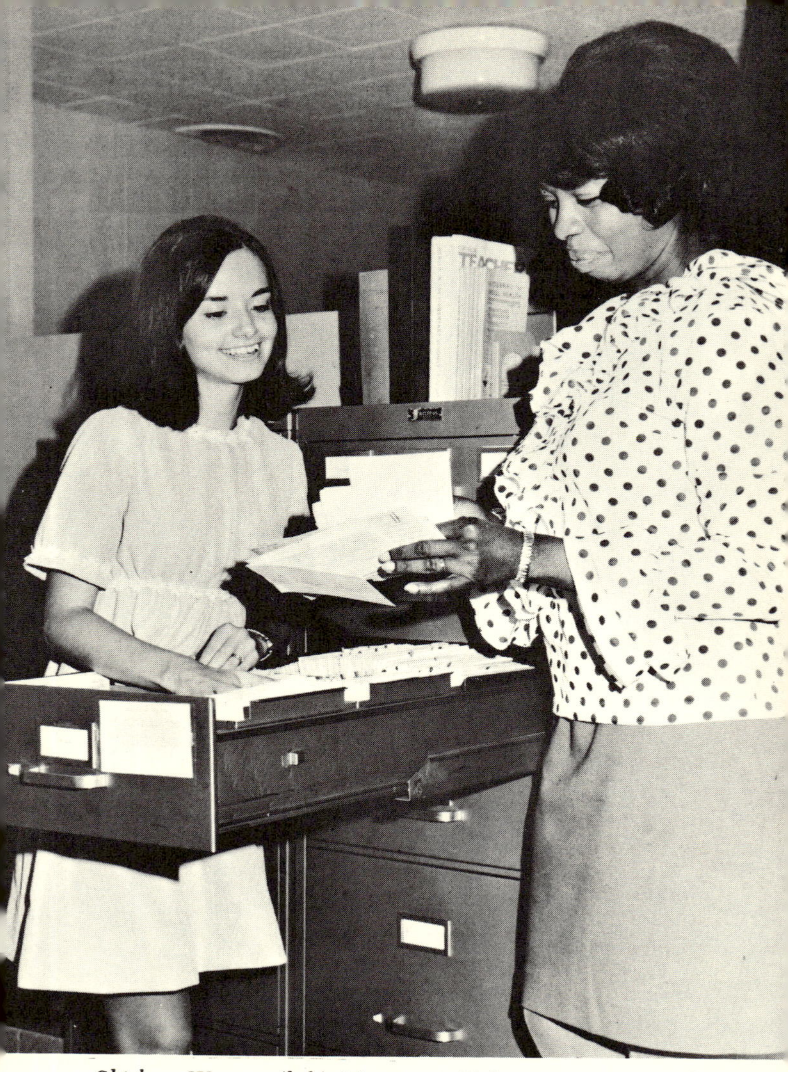

*Shirlene Wenger (left), Mennonite Voluntary Service work-
er in Los Angeles, California, goes over the filing with
school nurse, Mrs. Vidato.*

20

regeneration, but he always called for faith in Jesus as Savior and a commitment to do His will.

"Why should God make known His will if He would not will that a person do it?" Michael Sattler, another early Mennonite leader, asked. Faith and works could not be separated.

There Must Be Freedom of Religion

Since only mature adults could make this kind of commitment for life, the Mennonites did not baptize their children. God created children in love and would take care of them, even if they died, until they were old enough to make their own decision to follow or reject Jesus. But this meant freedom of religion, and voluntary church membership, which state authorities looked upon as treason.

The situation was not helped when Mennonites insisted that the state had no business telling the church what it should do. The church must be guided only by the Word of God and the Holy Spirit, they insisted. They saw no need for priests with special heavenly powers, for God, they believed, worked through each of His children. All believers are priests to each other and witnesses to society of what God is in Jesus Christ, they held.

Severe persecution followed. Many thousands were burned alive at the stake. Others were drowned, buried alive, or executed with the sword. One of the books describing what happened is the *Martyrs Mirror* with 1176 pages.

Those who survived found places of refuge and learned to keep their faith quietly to themselves.

Even today, when Mennonites think of who they are, they cannot forget the suffering of their fathers. This often makes others feel that they do not belong, even though they may believe as Mennonites do. But this is wrong, for those who share the history of faith in Christ and obedience to His will belong together, whether they are physical descendants of the Anabaptists or not.

Mennonites continued to migrate from country to country even after persecution ceased, however, because of their conscience against participating in any form of military service. A disciple of Jesus, they believed, should help to heal the wounds of individuals and nations rather than inflict death and destruction. The variety of practices among Mennonites of the same faith today is due largely to the different environments groups moved to in the course of time.

One major difference, however, came about through a division. In the 1690s a young elder, Jacob Ammon, in Switzerland and Alsace (France), led a group "back to the faith of the fathers," which he believed the more progressive Mennonites were forsaking. This group became known as the Amish, whose conservatism in dress and style of life is an attempt to be faithful to the ancient vision of the apostolic church.

In today's world of violence and technological progress, the simple life of the Amish seems wiser to many than they have been given credit

22

Amish children often attend one-room country schools. The Amish are wary of public schools and depend on church and home to instill proper values in their children.

Sunday morning worshipers at the Nyarusurya Mennonite Church in Tanzania.

Pastor D. A. Sonwani, Bishop O. P. Lal, and Bishop P. J. Malagar provide spiritual leadership to Mennonite churches around Bihar, India.

24

A Mennonite Disaster Service volunteer removes mud and debris from a flooded home in the aftermath of a hurricane that inundated Wilkes-Barre, Pennsylvania. In recent years many people who have suffered disasters have for the first time met Mennonites and Amish who came to help in the clean-up process.

The Amish practice mutual aid within their communities. If a barn burns down, fellow members provide the manpower and skill to erect a new one within a few days.

for. They are good farmers who were concerned for ecology long before it became fashionable. They do not become public charges financially. They pay their taxes. Most of their young people become model citizens and neighbors. They give generously to help the poor around the world and at home.

It is hard for the Amish to change. After all, they believe, the Bible and God's will do not change.

In the Name of Christ

About one half of the Mennonites and Amish in the world today live in North America, where the first groups arrived in 1683. By 1688 some of them were involved with the Quakers in drawing up one of the earliest protests against slavery issued in America. But until the twentieth century most of them were content to live quietly in their own communities.

Urbanization, mass media, technology has changed all that. Hundreds of Mennonite missionaries are scattered around the nations of the world as fraternal workers with national churches. At any given time some 800 Mennonite young people are serving abroad under the Mennonite Central Committee in education in Africa, community help projects in Bolivia, emergency relief in Bangladesh and Vietnam, and similar projects in over thirty countries. Non-Mennonite young people are joining them in service abroad and in the cities of North America as an alternative to violence.

Today many Mennonites, like the Amish,

Most Amish rely on horse-drawn buggies for their trans-
portation. Here a funeral procession heads for a plain
burial ground surrounded by open farmland. To the credit
of the Amish people, they remain entirely independent of
the government. They pay their taxes and obey the law,
but they see to it that none of their people ever go on
relief or in any way become a burden to society.

Hiroshi Kaneko serves as missionary director of the Japanese division at Radio HCJB, Quito, Ecuador, under appointment of the Japan Mennonite Church.

Takanori Sasaki (left), a former Japanese policeman, helps pour concrete at a Mennonite project in Germany, before enrolling in a Mennonite Bible School in Switzerland.

still wish to be left alone, but for different reasons; not to live simply, but to enjoy all the benefits of our affluent Western culture. Fortunately, however, many have caught a new vision of what the people of God are called to be and become, and are joining hands in a great effort to be faithful to the call of Jesus to follow Him.

Mennonites know they have no monopoly on the truth or the kingdom and rejoice with all who join them in the struggle for social justice, economic equality, and peace. They invite all who will respond to join the procession of those who really try to follow Jesus as Savior and as Lord.

Cornelius J. Dyck, *Executive Secretary*
Mennonite World Conference Presidium
Collegeville, Minnesota

Prologue

I hear the voice of God like silent songs
When evening comes to all the world,
And every field I've ever tilled
    (and that's a lot)
Lifts up a music all its own.

For He is there when I awake and when I
   go to sleep;
His voice, I hear it every day;
Yeah, even in the fields, around the world
Wherever I have gone — in Germany and
   Russia,
Penn's Woods, Ontario, Congo, and in Brazil;
Wherever I have fled
With nothing but a pocketful of grain,
His voice is there before I step ashore,
And singing plows the furrow,
Plants the seeds, and waits for fruit.

And if the harvest fails
In famine, death, and moving on,
God's voice goes on before
And I bring nothing but the seed
   (and hope)
That other men may hear that voice
And find a promise in that song.

1

"Hello," she said, smiling.

"Hi. What's your name?" he asked.

"My name is One-of-These," she said. "And yours?"

He turned away from her. "I have no name."

"You have no people then?"

"No people and no God."

She took his hand and turned him gently toward the light of the fire. "I'm sorry," she said. "I once had no people, and I know how you must feel. Come eat with us."

"No."

"But you are hungry."

"I don't need their food."

"It's our food, and yours too, if you need it."

"I'll eat with you then. I don't trust them and I don't need them. I've found my own way for a long time. So don't push me into their circle."

"I'm sorry."

"I don't mean to be rude. It's just that I've tried groups and they don't work for me. Besides, you're lovely enough for me. Let's you and me eat alone."

She smiled at him. "Come with me."

They sat by the fire and ate. They'd never

met before. Her people were feasting in the distance.

"Where do you come from?" he asked.

"From God."

"From God? How can that be?"

"A miracle, we believe."

"But how'd it ever happen?"

"How does anything happen? How does one explain one's birth?"

He was mystified. "Your people just began? Out of nothing?"

"No, not nothing. We were born out of prayer and faith and blood," she said. "A lot of blood."

"It sounds painful," he said.

"It was. Very."

"*There was a lot of debating at first. It seemed all we had in common was the conviction that only believing adults should be members of the true church.*"

Birth at Schleitheim

The time:	*The place:*
1527	**SWITZERLAND**

I shall never forget it. It changed the world. Schleitheim, that is. And I knew then that God was with us.

We were hiding in a cave near the border of the canton. My good Hans had received word during the day that a brother was coming to hide with us, and Hans had gone down the river to meet him. The authorities were killing every Anabaptist they could lay their hands on. It was terrifying, and I told Hans to be careful. "We lost the children," I told him. "So let's not lose each other."

"God will take care of us," he had said.

I sat in the cave, warming a stew for Hans and George and the new man. George had arrived two days ago. He too had wanted to attend the meeting at Schleitheim. But it had been impossible.

"I was in Zurich that day in January when Brother Felix was drowned, Elizabeth," George said as he warmed himself by the fire.

"You were?" I was surprised. I didn't know

how long George had been a true believer. "I hear he died singing, George," I said. "Is it true?"

"He cried out in praise to our Lord as he was bound with the ropes. I never saw anything like it, Elizabeth. The joy of the Lord triumphs over death!"

I smiled at George and gave him a cup of stew. He was a kind man, if one can judge kindness in two days. But a fiery determination lay beneath his kindness.

"Hans met Felix and Brother Conrad almost a year ago," I told him. "Hans said Felix was a wonderful man. They met in a cave similar to this one."

"They were both men of God."

"And now they're both dead." I couldn't keep the disappointment from my voice. "Our best leaders are gone, George, and the movement's only two years old."

"Faith, Elizabeth, faith! We have many good leaders like Michael Sattler. God is working out His will, and we are His servants. We must seek His purpose."

George finished his stew and I ate a bit myself. The cave was a miserable home. I hoped we could soon find a place more comfortable.

I thought of the children a lot. I wondered if they were still alive. They had been seized in an early morning raid several weeks ago in a village to the south, and I had not seen them since.

George stood up suddenly, pointing toward the door. "What was that noise?" he asked me.

36

We listened. I could hear nothing at first. Then I heard coughing.

"Elizabeth," a voice called.

I could feel my heart pounding. Who would know my name? No one but Hans.

"Hans?" I whispered back.

"It's me, wife." Hans stepped into the light near the entrance and came toward us, holding the arm of another man who was with him. "I brought Wolfgang," he said.

I was glad. "Thank God, you're safe."

Wolfgang was a young man, tall and straggly with mud. He looked around. "So this is the cave?"

"Ever been here?" George asked.

"No. Brother Michael told me about it."

I helped Wolfgang sit near the fire and brought him some hot stew. Hans said he hadn't eaten for two days.

"From where do you come, Wolfgang?" George asked.

"Schleitheim, at the border."

Hans put a blanket around his shoulders. "Wolfgang attended the conference there, George."

"He did! What happened? I've been praying for it for weeks, hoping God would bring these many believers together as one."

I was very excited. I too, had prayed for the meeting.

"He says Michael was used of the Lord in a powerful way," Hans whispered to me.

"It was the greatest experience of my life," Wolfgang said between gulps.

"What happened?" George asked, moving closer.

"There was a lot of debating at first. It seemed all we had in common was the conviction that only believing adults should be members of the true church."

"Adult baptism," George nodded.

I didn't usually join in such conversations, but I couldn't hide my curiosity. "So it all ended up in disagreement then?"

"No, no, Elizabeth," Wolfgang replied, turning to me. He paused as he handed me his cup. "Thanks for the food. It was wonderful." I took the cup and filled it again.

"Things have developed so fast with our movement," he continued. "Well, you know that. It's only two years since we broke with Zwingli and the other reformers. It's no wonder, with all the persecution, that we haven't been able to come to a common understanding of our faith."

Hans shook his head. He was a wise man, even if I say so myself. And by the troubled look on his face, I knew he hoped that Schleitheim was more than another debate.

"But a miracle happened!" Wolfgang exclaimed, standing to his feet, joy in his face. "I never in my life saw so many people together, agreeing in the Lord. There were the fanatics who thought we should seize power and use the sword like Zwingli and Luther and Rome. There were the spiritualists who suggested that we should deny the Bible's revelation. There were the conformists who urged us to reunite with Zwingli. Oh, Hans, I tell you, there were so many different groups, I almost left.

"But then Michael preached. It was a fantastic sermon. God visited us; that's the best way I can explain it. God's Spirit moved among us and brought us together and our understanding was drafted and accepted without a single person's contradiction!"

I was crying I was so happy. George was embracing Wolfgang and Hans took me in his strong arms and kissed me over and over. "God has saved us," he said. "Thank the Lord for Schleitheim."

We were still filthy, weary, and half-starved, our children were lost, and the future was uncertain. But we fell on our knees around the fire and prayed our thanks. God had saved us. And things would never be the same.

Five and forty decades of gathering and scat-
    tering
The Lord is my shepherd, I shall not want
gathering and scattering all over the world
I shall not want
pursuing and pursued
He maketh me to lie down
He leadeth me
nicknamed and drowned in mockery of the
    water of faith
Green pastures and still waters
confessing a new way of living
and giving and believing and hoping
He restoreth my soul
seeking for the promised land
He leadeth me
praying that reunion time may come — soon
Paths of righteousness, for His name's sake
alone in the face of the future
alone with the blood of the past
Yea, though I walk through the valley of the
    shadow of death,
I will fear no evil, for Thou art with me:
Thy rod and Thy staff they comfort me
alone together in the present age, caught and
    yet free

40

Table in the presence of mine enemies
five and forty decades of cowardice and
   courage
My head with oil — my cup
faith and doubt
Cup runneth over
Amen
Surely
Amen and amen
*Surely goodness and mercy shall follow me all
   the days of my life,*
*And I will dwell in the house of the Lord
   forever*
Amen
Forever
Reunion time forever. Amen.

"Are your people all the same kind?" he asked when they had finished eating.

She smiled at him across the fire.

"Why do you smile? Is it a silly question?" he asked.

"No. I'm smiling because you ask difficult questions, not silly ones. You see, in the beginning we were a motley group. Many different kinds of people."

"What brought you together?"

"Not what. Who."

He shook his head. "I'm lost," he said.

"God brought us together," she said simply.

"Of course God did. But what forces or ideas?"

"We believed we could be God's people in a new way."

He moved closer, studying her, wanting to kiss her beautiful face, but resisting the urge. "Did it work?"

"Sure."

"I mean, did you really become what you wanted to be?" he persisted.

"Only God knows. For me, it's so much better than trying to make it by myself."

He looked toward the distance where her

people were camped. "What are those big fires on the horizon?" he asked. "Are they offering sacrifices?"

She turned quickly and looked where he pointed, a cry of anguish deep in her bosom as she rose to her feet. She started running toward the fires in the distance, her arms reaching toward heaven, her voice lost in the wind. Then she stopped and sank to her knees.

He went after her. Her lips were moving but her voice was silent.

He took her in his arms and carried her back to their fire. He kissed her tears and put his coat about her. The fire was low.

He waited for her to speak. Her crying had stopped and her face was quiet. He turned to look at the distance. The fires were gone.

"What happened?" he asked.

"We must give thanks," she said.

"Give thanks?"

"Some of my brothers and sisters have entered their rest, and we must thank God for saving them. Much as I hate the stake, we must give thanks."

"You mean they were burning people over there?"

"My people."

"But who did it?"

"Them."

"Who's them?"

"The world." She kissed him gently. "Thanks for taking care of me," she said. "Come now, let's give thanks."

"You do it," he said. "I'm not used to it."

Anneken smiled. "I'll be all right now, Dirk. God brought you just in time. Were you in prison?"

Rape or Execution?

<table>
<tr><td>The time:
1540</td><td>The place:
THE NETHERLANDS</td></tr>
</table>

Anneken was a sick girl. Sick and troubled. She had not seen her parents for months. Perhaps they were dead. But Anneken persisted in hope. Hope that they would yet be reunited. Hope that the persecution would go away. Hope that Dirk her lover was still alive.

Too many had already died. The authorities had become frightened since Münster, and they killed many of the believers they captured. They now were convinced that all Anabaptists were radical fanatics. Some of the Anabaptists had taken up the sword and proclaimed themselves the new Zion. They had killed and conquered in the name of Christ. Now everyone was suspect.

Anneken had been in prison herself. The fever had begun in that diseased place, and had haunted her ever since. She was a healthy, attractive young woman, but the fever had already left its mark. Some days she wished for death, when the days got longer than the nights.

Just three short years before, she had lived

with her parents in the city. Her father was important, and they had lived well. People respected them. Now they were considered common criminals and were hunted everywhere they went. Following their new faith meant literally giving up everything.

At first Anneken found it exciting to join the small band of believers who sought to be the true church. It gave her new energy, new life. And she liked the people. That's how she met Dirk. But now the novelty was gone. Death stood not far away, watching. She never heard from Dirk and Anneken feared her prayers were mere whispers in the night.

Gertrude was kind to keep her here in her house. It was dangerous. Gertrude had not yet been suspected by the authorities, but Anneken was sure Gertrude was a believer too.

"Anneken, you must not let your spirits drop," Gertrude told her when she came to her room today. "You must be brave and strong."

Anneken sat up on her elbow as Gertrude changed the bedding. Gertrude's family was wealthy too. Anneken watched her work and marveled at her ability with manual chores.

"I'm afraid," Anneken said.

"Don't be. Just be thankful you escaped."

"Thankful? Gertrude, how can you say that? I'm on the edge of collapse and you tell me to give thanks!"

Gertrude smiled faintly as she helped Anneken lie down again. "God will protect us, Anneken, I believe it. Didn't you hear about the brothers and sisters who escaped from prison in

Amsterdam? Only God could have worked such a miracle."

Neither woman noticed a young man, tattered and dirty, enter the room. "I see your faith never wavers, Gertrude," he said wearily.

Anneken sat up and in one sweeping movement was out of bed and running into his arms. "Dirk! God has saved you!" He took her feverish body in his arms and kissed her. It was a strange sight — lovers reunited, both exhausted and fighting for life.

"I love you, Anneken," he said.

"I love you." Anneken's face was already full of new life. "Oh, darling, where have you been?"

He helped her into bed. "Never mind, Anneken, we are together at last." He sat by her side, her hand wrapped around his.

"Anneken is a sick girl, Dirk," Gertrude said.

"I could see it the moment I entered. Darling, you are so pale. What is it?"

"The fever."

Anneken smiled. "I'll be all right now, Dirk. God brought you just in time. Were you in prison?"

"I was condemned with a group of brothers and sisters to a cold tower, where we were sentenced to bread and water and total darkness until death. Some got sick and died. And in that terrible darkness we living walked and slept among the dead. Until one day two of the men lost their heads and attacked the guard, and all of us who could went out to see the light. Except several who said it was wrong to escape."

"Did they kill the guard?" Anneken asked.

"I don't think so. I couldn't see much after days of absolute darkness. I just walked out."

"Oh, darling, I'm so glad you're here. Gertrude will help you clean up. You didn't see my parents anywhere, did you, Dirk?"

"No, Jan and Menno told me about them. I'm so sorry. But I'm thankful you escaped, Anneken."

"You saw Menno?"

"Yes, two weeks ago. Near the bridge on the north side of Groningen. He is such a great man!"

"Is he well?"

"I've seen him better. His wife is not well, you know. But the man's faith is really something."

Anneken was sitting up in bed again, stroking Dirk's hand, her face troubled with worry. "Menno has been under such stress with all the radical revolutionaries resorting to force to achieve what they think is God's kingdom. Menno must be torn between them and the pagan traditions of Rome."

Dirk put his arms around her again and hugged her. Gertrude left the room, and for a moment each forgot the trouble and disease. For a moment they were just the two they used to be before the fire of persecution had burned so wide a path. He kissed her and laid her head back on her pillow.

"Take care of yourself, precious one," he whispered. "God will lead us to the promised land someday soon."

48

As he stood up, Anneken reached up and clasped his hand against her lips. "Dirk, you didn't kill the guard at the tower, did you?"

"I said I couldn't even see — two men jumped him."

"But you didn't help, did you?"

Dirk shook his head. "I pushed the door open, Anneken."

She smiled. "There's nothing wrong with that."

"I don't think so either." He stood. "I better get some clean clothes. I'll be back."

Anneken watched him leave the room. She sang softly to herself, lost in a reverie of used to be and will be, trying to forget the fever and the fires. But a sadness crept into her tone, and she sighed and closed her eyes.

She was asleep when he came back. He sat beside her bed and watched her. Her face stirred with her dream, and suddenly she jerked awake, fear in her eyes. He held her close and comforted her.

"I'm afraid, Dirk."

"Don't be."

"But what if the authorities find you?"

"Anneken, I don't wish to be a martyr. If I can escape without hurting anyone, without the use of force, I'll escape. I'm not like some of those brothers and sisters at the prison who could have walked out into the light but didn't. I'm not seeking death, but I'm not afraid of death, either."

"I wish I were well so I could go with you."

"Don't be silly. Gertrude will take good care

of you. And the authorities will not bother you as long as you're sick."

"But I want to be well!"

"You will be soon, darling, I believe it."

Anneken hugged Dirk, suddenly happy and relieved. His faith had always inspired her.

Gertrude came running into the room. "Dirk, there are soldiers coming!"

"Are you sure?" Dirk asked, rushing toward the door.

"I'm sure."

"Are you positive they're coming here to your house?"

"Not absolutely, but it looks that way."

Dirk squared his shoulders and looked at Anneken. "You two don't get excited. Trust God, darling. Lie down and try to relax. Gertrude, go out in the other room. I believe it's best for me to stay here, in case they are going on up the street. I'm hiding under the bed. It's the last place they'll look."

"I love you, darling."

"Sh. Just pray that God may work His will."

Anneken lay back in her bed and tried to look calm. "Oh God, save us," she breathed. She heard soldiers in the outer room. Gertrude was trying to reason with them, but their voices were getting louder. Suddenly they burst into her room and came marching over to her bed.

"Where is your boyfriend?" the big one shouted, grabbing her by the hair and shaking her head till she thought the hair would tear from its roots. She screamed without realizing it.

50

The other soldier was half drunk and he sat beside her with a wicked smile on his face, the stench from his breath and his beard almost worse than the pain.

The big soldier slapped her. "I'm in a rush, woman. My orders are to find that Dirk before the sun rises again, and if I don't, I'm supposed to bring you in."

The drunk soldier grinned. "After we're finished with her!"

Anneken screamed. "Take your hands off me."

The drunk seized her and pulled her out of bed, throwing her to the floor. "Don't you talk like that to the captain, you heretic-lover." He stood over her and hiccuped, laughing gleefully. "Which one do you want, captain? The sick one might have a disease, but then again she might be pretending."

Gertrude started toward him. "God will strike you dead."

The big soldier grabbed Gertrude and threw her back against the wall. "Shut up, or we'll take you along."

The drunk soldier giggled. "God will strike me dead, will He? I'd be dead a hundred times if that were so." He drew his sword and pointed it at Anneken, crouching on the floor beneath him. "Up, woman."

Anneken trembled. She'd heard of such men. In the old days, a man would have been hung for speaking to her in such a way. But this was different. She must keep them from discovering Dirk.

"I said stand up!" he yelled. She moved slowly, her eyes on the sword. It was sharp, she could see. She could feel the blood rushing in her head.

"Now take those clothes off."

She was horrified. "No, I will not," she stammered.

"I think I'll take this one, captain. She looks delicious!" The soldier staggered after Anneken as she backed away. Maybe she could coax them out of the room. But he cornered her, his sword close to her throat.

"I'm not joking, whore," he said. "You let me see that body of yours or I'll rip those clothes off myself and we'll burn the house and the clothes together."

Anneken was trapped. The fever swelled in her head and she tried to think. She could not let this man go on. Nor could she betray Dirk. She was caught between betrayal and betrayal.

The soldier cut the loop in her nightgown, and she reached up to catch it, gripping it close to her neck. She could feel the blade on her breast as he cut the cloth away, blood oozing down her bare skin. She clasped at her clothes trying to cover herself, trying to hide. But his sword came back, cutting her hand, slicing away the nightgown. He was roaring with hungry laughter as he stripped her, his knife nicking her skin as he slashed back and forth. She shrieked as she turned away, crouching against the wall, naked and shivering.

Then he grabbed her. His slimy, cold hand gripped her feverish shoulder and spun her around. She was shamed. She was sobbing as she fell to the floor, her arms trying to shield her breasts from the drunken beast.

Anneken barely remembered the rest. Dirk came roaring from under the bed, his anger hot with grief in his face. "Take me, take me," he shouted. "And don't touch these women. And may God forgive you."

They took him away. Anneken remembered only his anguished face as they pulled him through the doorway. "I love you, darling," he called. "I love you. God keep you safe."

Gertrude rushed over with a blanket and helped Anneken back into bed. She washed her cuts and bathed her throbbing head.

Anneken fell into a fitful sleep and slept for days. She dreamed she saw Dirk standing in the promised land, waving for her to come join the pilgrims. And when she went to go, a sword stopped her.

When she awakened, she was alone with Gertrude, as before. There was no word of Dirk. The villagers did say that a dozen Anabaptists were burned at the stake in the valley that night. But no one knew who. At least they weren't telling.

Anneken was weaker than before. But her faith persisted. She still hoped that they would be reunited. And Gertrude hoped with her.

Good-bye, farewell, my love,
My heart weeps not in fear;
God keep you strong and grant you peace
Across that mighty flood
Until reunion time.
Farewell.
Remember all the promises
And don't forget, my love,
Death cannot be the enemy
If love goes on before.
Farewell.

The sun was up before they awakened. Her people were already breaking camp. Some were marching east, shouting to others to follow.

She heard the shouts and rose from her pillow. She washed herself and dressed. Then she went to awaken him. He sat up abruptly, fear in his face. "Where are we?" he asked.

"We're here, and we'll soon be there," she said, kissing him. "Come, let's be going."

"I'm tired of always moving on," he said, crawling from his bed. "Why don't we settle down someplace."

"We will," she said. "God has promised us that much."

"But when?"

"Soon. Here, let me wash you. We must hurry or we'll be left behind."

"I prefer to keep my distance from your people," he said. "They get on my nerves. Besides, I'm not one of them. I don't have to do what they say."

She sang to herself as she washed him clean. Her hands soothed his aches and warmed his shivering body. "I love you," she whispered as she finished.

"I appreciate that," he said, grinning as he

55

dressed. He wrapped their packs and shared a loaf of bread with her. "Seriously, though, how do I know you aren't just trying to trick me into loving your people?"

She was hurt, and her face showed it. "I do love you," she said. "I'll leave my people if you ask me."

"How could you do that? You'd lose your name."

She watched her people moving toward the east. "How can I show you my love?" she asked.

"You have already," he said, kissing her. "It's just that your people give me the creeps."

She took the packs and headed west. "Let's leave them then."

He ran after her and stopped her. "No, it won't work," he said.

"Why not?"

"Because you love God as much as you love me. And your people are God's family to you. You need them."

"I know."

"Then let's go with them, but keep our distance."

"How can you know what they're like if you

never mix with them?" she asked.

"I get close enough," he said. "Close enough to see that God's people do less loving than they say they do."

"That's why we stick together," she said.

"You seek a full belly," Cornelius said firmly, "and I seek a free conscience. Conscience is always first."

The Conscience and the Belly

Cornelius Penner did not want to leave Chortitza. Nor did his family. But God was beckoning them, he believed. To a land he'd never seen, far beyond the Russian border. And like Abraham, Cornelius was answering God's mysterious call.

They were leaving today. Cornelius came from the farmyard, pulling a cart, quickly and with determination in his step. His father had come to the Ukraine four decades before. Four decades, two years, and ten months. In search of food and new peace. Now, as thousands were still arriving from Prussia, Cornelius was leaving the Old Colony. Many of his neighbors laughed at him. But that didn't stop Cornelius.

"Elfrieda!" He parked the cart by the gate and looked toward the house. He called again. "Elfrieda."

A young girl came running, a small box in her arms.

"Sara, where's your mother?"

"She's in the house, Papa," the girl said. She was about fifteen, with a little nose and big eyes.

She handed her father the small box. "Why do
you shout so loud?"

"I'm in a hurry."

"Aren't we all?"

"Besides, young lady, I wasn't shouting. You
should know better than to scold your father."
He loaded a second box, a big one, heaving it
in place with the strength of two men.

The girl was not frightened by her father.
"I'm sorry, Papa," she said. "I thought you wanted us to leave unnoticed. But you sure fuss a
lot."

Cornelius turned to her with a warning in
his eyes. But his attention was drawn away by
his wife coming down the path from the
house. "Mother, what's taking you so long?"

"You know, Cornelius," she said, ignoring his
question, "I've come to love Russia."

"Shush! No one loves Russia."

"Oh, but I do," Sara joined in. "I'm anxious
to go to America, but I'll miss Chortitza."

Cornelius softened his tone. "Mother Russia,
they say — and so it is. My parents brought
me here as a baby — but now I take my leave."

"I'll miss the house," his wife said.

"I'll miss the fields," Cornelius said.

"I'll miss my friends," their daughter said. The
three of them paused for a moment beside the
cart, looking out across the village.

"Did you speak to Uncle Peter, Papa?"

"Yes, he knows."

Elfrieda nodded. "Everyone knows."

"We're leaving Russia, and God knows too,"
Sara said. She watched her mother lift a pack-

age onto the cart. Elfrieda was a big woman, strong, broad-shouldered, and bosomy.

"What's it like in America, Mama?"

"A wilderness."

Cornelius nodded grimly. "Full of savages, Sara."

"Then why are we going, Papa?"

"They say it's a land of promise."

"Who's they?"

"You know, like Canaan."

"Then why aren't the other Mennonites going?"

Elfrieda sighed. "Too much milk and honey here, Sara."

They worked at wrapping their past and packing it on their little cart. Excitement mixed with gloom. Hope with fear.

"What'll become of the house, Cornelius? Will the *Russe* confiscate it?"

Sara leaned on the gate, watching the big house. "They take away our right not to kill," she said. "Will they also burn our house and take away our right to live?"

Cornelius tried to reassure his child. "Perhaps one of the Mennonite families arriving from Prussia will get our house. Perhaps one of my cousins will harvest the crops."

"But Papa, why do we leave when others are only arriving?"

"We must leave while we can, Sara."

Elfrieda nodded. "The czar doesn't like us as much as Catherine did."

"Catherine's long gone, Elfrieda. Times are changing. They're taking away our privileges."

Sara was not convinced. She helped her father lift a box into place and then stood staring for a long time. "The harvest looks good, Papa," she said.

His answer came quickly, almost too quickly. "The harvest is always ahead of us, never behind us," he said, laying a hand on her shoulder. "Don't you ever forget that, Sara."

Elfrieda brought a chair and Cornelius tied it on the top of the load. Sara stood off to one side, near the garden gate, her hands deep in her pockets as she fought the tears.

"Peter says we shall meet the children at the border," Cornelius was saying to Elfrieda between grunts as he pulled the rope tight.

"I do hope they're safe."

"He says they're fine. I pray God no evil comes to them." He put on his coat and walked briskly to the barn for a last glance around. He loved the farm. But he did not linger long. Cornelius never lingered long after his mind was made up.

"Let's be going," he said abruptly. "We'll take the back way."

Elfrieda turned suddenly to Sara as though she had almost forgotten something. "Go get the bag under the hidden stones," she instructed.

"Yes, Mama." Sara was glad for an excuse to go back to the house.

Elfrieda sighed as Cornelius put on his gloves. "One must be careful with the German Bible."

"One must be careful, but not too careful," he said.

Sara came running from the big house with

tears in her eyes. She did not look back. "Is it really necessary to act so secretive about this?"

"Yes, Sara child," Elfrieda said as she took the package and hid it under the boxes. "One must be careful, but not too careful."

Cornelius smiled at his wife. Then he turned to Sara, and put his arm about her shoulders in a gesture of comfort. "Some follow their bellies, Sara, but we must follow God."

"God doesn't care whether we have enough to eat?"

"Of course He does. He always takes care of His own."

Cornelius began to pull the cart. "Come now, let's be going."

Sara ran her fingers along the gate and looked at everything, trying to drink in every last detail and store it in the forever of her soul. "Farewell," she whispered.

"You were born in that house," Elfrieda said as she too lingered behind.

"I know."

"I almost feel as though I was too."

"It was a nice house — and a happy home."

Cornelius was already on the road. "We must keep moving," he called. They hurried to catch up. "Don't talk so much," he scolded.

"Will we ever really settle down, Papa?"

He didn't answer. Nor did Elfrieda, who was worried about the other children.

They moved quickly along the road as the day passed. Many of the neighbors were in the fields and did not notice the Penners leaving the Old Colony. And those who did see them waved indifferently and chatted among themselves as they watched the Penners go by. Obviously, no one else was as disturbed about their adopted homeland as Cornelius was.

Sara and her mother talked a lot as they went. They both loved Chortitza, and they knew they'd never be back.

They soon left the village and started across the long miles of countryside. West. Toward America.

"The fields are so vast and comforting," Sara mused. "That's Russia, Mama, like late afternoon rain in a dry spring."

Elfrieda looked out across the fields. "Russia — is it dry or is it spring?"

Cornelius sighed as he listened to the women talking. Once when they stopped to rest, he said, "I never knew women could talk so much."

Elfrieda laughed. "You must never have met your own mother, Cornelius. She had a good tongue, if good means a lot."

"Your talking will get you in trouble, woman."

"My talking and your grumbling."

Sara came running from the other side of the road. "Look, Papa. What's that down the road?"

"It looks like someone coming this way."

"I see two people."

"Two people and a wagon."

Sara tugged at his arm. "Shall we hide, Papa?"

"No. Just hold still. It may be a family from Prussia. I heard several were coming soon."

As the two people came closer, Cornelius saw

they were a man and a woman with packs on their shoulders, weary with travel.

"Are we going the wrong way?" the stranger called.

"Depends where you're going, friend."

"We're seeking the promised land, so to speak."

"You're heading the wrong way," Cornelius answered.

"We're on our way to Chortitza."

"I said you're heading the wrong way."

The stranger came closer. "Is that so? Who, may I ask, is of that opinion?"

"I am, my friend. Cornelius Penner, formerly of Chortitza, now headed for America with my wife, Elfrieda, my daughter Sara, and my four younger children who await us near the border."

"Penner? My name is Epp, David Epp. This is my wife, Helene. We are fresh from Prussia where land is scarce and living is hard."

Cornelius stepped forward and extended his hand. "I believe we are cousins, David. Cousins in the flesh, but not in the spirit perhaps."

The stranger put down his pack and shook hands. "How do you mean that?"

"You seek a full belly," Cornelius said firmly, "and I seek a free conscience."

Elfrieda broke in. "But Cornelius, that's not fair. We wouldn't be going to America if we expected to starve."

The stranger was amused. "You seek a free conscience and a full belly then?"

"You might say that," Cornelius conceded. "But conscience is always first."

The stranger's wife came forward, her face pale and dirty under the rags she was wearing. "Many have written to us of happiness and prosperity here in Russia."

"No doubt. Our people are prosperous, after many hard years. But the belly can consume the soul, cousin."

The stranger grunted aloud. "Perhaps you're right. I'll be better able to judge that when my belly is full once again. We've been in hard times."

"Very hard," the woman said. "Some starved."

Cornelius saw the day was late. "I bid you God's peace, Cousin David. We must be going." He went back to the cart and turned to the Epps as they adjusted their packs and moved on toward the village. "I wish you a good harvest," he called. "And I hope you give thanks."

"Oh, we will."

The women waved to each other. "The Lord is good," Cornelius called.

"The Lord is good," the answer came back. They waved again, like pilgrims silhouetted against the wilderness and the road. And then they turned and each continued on their journey to the promised land.

Where goes this road?
    Our conscience tells us not,
Yet we must go.
When comes our rest?
    How soon the promised land
We do not know.
And yet we go
    Our feet upon the road,
    For God has promised us a day
    When conscience shall find peace.
And we shall be at home
    Along that road, one day,
    And we shall rest with joy.

"Let's go in," she said.

"I can't. I know they won't accept me," he said.

They sat looking down across the village in the valley below. Neat little houses, row on row. All the same. Or nearly.

"They've settled down," she said. "And now you don't want to settle down, do you?"

"I've nothing against settling down," he replied. "It's just that I don't want to build a house exactly like theirs. My house would be different."

On the far side of the settlement a young family had built a smaller house with more windows and a roof peaked at a different angle.

"I like that house," he said, pointing. "That family has pride. And a sense of belonging together. They built a house that makes them distinctive."

"But the whole village is distinctive. That's the main reason we've been traveling for so long. We wanted to get away from those fires, those burnings at the stake, and find a valley where we could be God's people of love, without perishing."

"Look," he said, pointing again.

The house with the windows and the funny roof was burning. Villagers were standing around watching while others drove the young family from the settlement. The roof collapsed as the house crumbled under the flames.

"That's why I won't go in," he said. "Fire is fire."

There were tears in her eyes as they watched. "I never thought it would come to this," she said. "We forget love so soon. It's a new kind of world."

"And your name is still One-of-These?"

"Yes. We must go into the village and speak peace," she said.

"You go. They are not my people," he said. He kissed her.

"Please come along."

He shook his head. "I won't be burned in the name of love," he said.

Four years had changed a lot, and they weren't sure how to be brothers. Neither knew how to close the gap.

Samuel Comes Home

"Hello, Mother."

Singing to herself as she knit by the kitchen fire, she had not heard him enter. She turned abruptly in her rocking chair, surprise in her face.

"Samuel." Her tone was part question, part hope. Caught for a moment between sitting and standing, she studied his face in the late afternoon shadows. "Samuel, is it you?"

"Sorry if I scared you, Mother." He stepped across the threshold, cap in hand. "Is Father here?"

Four years of waiting brought her rising out of the chair, the knitting falling to the floor as she rushed toward her son, her pale eyes singing and her tired face nervous with joy. *Welcome home, welcome home.* But just as quickly as fear follows joy, four years of waiting brought her feet to a stop, mere steps from her boy, her arms aching to embrace him and greet him.

He was embarrassed. She could see his face now, and his eyes looked away. Restraint battled hope in her bosom. She sought for her voice, her forehead quivering with emotion. But he moved away with an aloofness she'd never seen in her son.

"Father's not home then?"

She went back to her chair, still rocking with joy, and picked up the needles and wool. "He'll be back by nightfall. He's at the blacksmith."

"And the children?"

"Jakie's plowing. The girls are helping Aunt Esther. Father's going to be bringing them along home."

He touched the top of the table, testing its texture and strength. Getting reacquainted, reaching back to familiar memories. Four years of yesterdaying. Now home.

"Don't worry, Mother," he said, glancing about, avoiding her eyes as he examined her kitchen. "I'm not staying. I just happened to be coming this way. I'll have to be moving along shortly."

She didn't answer, going to the cupboard for some cake, pouring him some milk. *Maybe he'll stay. Please God, yes.*

She took him the food. "Are you well?" she asked, forcing her voice casual and low.

"Oh, yes. Yes, I'm well enough," he said, never looking at her as he took the cake and milk. He sat opposite the rocker and ate slowly, taking large bites, pretending he didn't need the food. She knew he was starved.

He wiped his mouth and handed her the glass. He looked at her this time, concern in his face. "And you — are you well, Mother?"

"As well as can be expected." Her voice broke. She hugged his head against her bosom, he sitting, she standing with face uplifted. Shadowed against the fire of the late day. "It's been so long, Samuel," she whispered.

"Yes, it has been, Mother."

She kissed him on the cheek. *Welcome home, son.* He didn't respond. He was embarrassed again. She could see it. She went to the cupboard for more cake.

"Jakie's getting married, you know," she said, her voice calm now.

"Jakie is! But isn't he too young?"

"He'll be twenty next month."

"Twenty! I can't believe it. He was barely sixteen when I left."

"Yes, I guess he would have been. It is nearly four years." She brought him the cake and watched him wolf it down as she rocked and knitted. "He's marrying Judith Yoder."

"Who's she?"

"Tobias Yoder's oldest."

"Toby has a daughter old enough for Jakie?"

"She's eighteen, and she's quite a mature woman for her age."

"No doubt." He finished the cake and wiped his mouth again. "Well, it sounds like Jakie's got himself a good Mennonite girl."

"They're nice people."

"I'm sure." He smiled for the first time, amused and not quite believing. "Will they be farming nearby?"

"It looks like they'll be working the old Swartzentruber place."

"Down the road?"

She looked up from her work and nodded. They sat silently then, her rocker motionless as she watched him. "How's Emily?"

"Emily?" Samuel looked at his mother, his face puzzled and vacant. "Oh, Emily!" Puzzlement left his face, bitterness rising with the blood and snapping eyes. He laughed an angry harshness, standing abruptly and pacing noisily about. "Did you ask me how Emily is, Mother?"

"Yes, I — I did." She sat forward in her chair, watching him apprehensively.

"I don't know."

"What?"

He roared at her. "I don't know, I said."

"You don't know?"

"I haven't seen her since you have."

"What?" The word was more of a cry than a question.

"I haven't seen her since you have, Mother, not since that cold night nearly four years ago when Father threw me out of this house and told me never to come back. I've never seen Emily since."

"But — But, Samuel — I thought you were married."

"Married!" He spit the words in her face as he bent toward the rocker, crouching over his mother like a mad animal. "What does it mean to be married, Mother?" he thundered. "I've been hunting for my wife, Emily, up and down this land for four years, and I've never seen her face. I've never heard her voice since she fled from this kitchen, her hands to her face, weeping

74

as Father bellowed his wrath on the two of us. I've never seen her, Mother, never. Is that what it means to be married?"

He straightened and walked away from her. She watched him go.

"I'm so sorry, Samuel," she said. "I didn't know." *Oh, God, forgive us.*

His voice was calculated now, like an echo over many years. "Don't be sorry, Mother. Just don't say anything, please. It's too late for sorrow, too late for pity. It's too late for anything, Mother. What's done is done. I fell in love with a beautiful girl who didn't understand our traditions. I was scared to ask Father's permission because I was sure I wouldn't get it. So I married Emily and brought her here for your blessing. But a father's wrath is hardly a blessing."

"Samuel, I had no idea."

"I know you didn't." He moved back toward his mother, searching the room to make sure no one was eavesdropping. "I don't hold it against you, Mother," he said. His tone made the meaning clear. She kept her eyes on her knitting, struggling to bring her son home without betraying his father. Her face was one of weathered beauty, strong and enduring as the prairie.

Silence fell between them as evening came in among the late afternoon gloom. She rose to stir the fire. "What have you been working at?" she asked Samuel.

"Whatever I could find, Mother." He seemed touched by her interest. "It's a hard world out there. I always thought the farm was hard, but

working in the steel mills and on the railroads
is no easy thing. I traveled a lot, hoping to find
Emily with one of her relatives."

They heard footsteps as Jakie entered from
the barn. Jakie was younger than Samuel, rather
handsome and a bit gangly and frail. His face
broke into a half smile as he stared at his older
brother. "Samuel, it's you, isn't it?"

Samuel rose and walked toward Jakie,
extending his hand cautiously. "Yeah,
Jakie, it's me all right." They shook. "How you
been, brother?"

"Pretty good. Are you here to talk to
Father?"

Samuel laughed nervously. "No, not really."

"You just passing through, then?"

"Yeah, Jakie, I guess you could say that."
Samuel continued to smile uncomfortably as his
brother watched him. Four years had changed
a lot, and they weren't sure how to be brothers.

"Hey, Jakie, Mother says you're getting married."

"Yeah," Jakie seemed pleased, but tried to
act nonchalant.

"Toby Yoder's daughter?"

"Yeah."

"Pretty nice young lady, huh?"

"Yeah."

"And you'll be farming the old Swartzentruber place?"

"Yeah."

They fell silent again, each a bit eager to
close the gap between them, but neither knowing how to do it. Jakie responded warmly, but

his tone held a safe distance. The mother listened carefully, praying they wouldn't quarrel. *Lord, give us peace.*

Samuel turned suddenly. "Mother, is Grandpa still alive?"

"He died last fall."

"He did?" His tone spoke his surprise and disappointment. "I was hoping to see him before I left. I always liked Grandpa." He walked to his mother, laying a hand on her shoulder. "I'm sorry."

"Grandma's not well either, son. She often asks about you."

"She does? She has so many grandchildren, she shouldn't worry about me."

"Samuel, she always says she hopes you come home someday."

"She does?"

"She said she thought you probably had children by now. And you know she doesn't like any of her children outside the church, son."

Samuel pulled his hand away. He turned so she couldn't see the answer in his face. His tone was level, but his eyes were angry. "Well, you can tell Grandma there's no children, Mother."

Jakie moved toward the door. "I hear horses. It's probably Father coming with the girls."

Samuel took his cap and began to button his coat as he paused by the rocker. "It was good to see you, Mother."

"Samuel, can't you stay?"

"It's out of the question."

Jakie came back toward them. "Samuel, Father

will forgive you if you treat him right."

"I doubt that, Jakie," Samuel said, taking his brother's hand and shaking it hard. "Good-bye. Tell the girls I said hello. I'm not dead as Father would have me. I'm not happy either, but I am alive. And as long as I'm still alive, there's hope of finding Emily." Jakie held his hand long after they had finished shaking, trying to persuade him to stay. But Samuel drew away. "Good-bye, Mother," he said.

"Samuel, please stay and speak to your father."

"Why, Mother? What's to gain?"

"You could come home again."

"A son who is thrown from his father's house can never come home again. Never. Good-bye."

She kept on rocking, but the firmness in her voice turned to pleading. "Samuel, what is there out there in the world that keeps pulling you away from us?"

He looked at her as Jakie stood beside her, silhouetted against the low fire. He loved her, but his anger denied it. "Nothing keeps pulling me away from you, Mother, nothing. Not even Emily." His voice softened. "Mother, I didn't pull away. I was cut off."

"I never wanted it that way."

"I know, Mother, I know. I don't hold it against you." Jakie watched helplessly as Samuel turned to the door.

"Why are you so proud?" he cried out suddenly. "Samuel, why are you too proud to ask Father's forgiveness?"

78

"I'm not proud, Jakie. I'm just realistic," Samuel said quickly, as though brushing it aside. His tone became confidential. "Besides, I'm not sure the old man knows how to forgive."

"Do you?"

The brothers used to romp together and tell each other secrets no one ever knew. Now they were men, standing in their mother's kitchen, wrestling with each other's motives, worlds apart.

"I hear the horses at the barn," Samuel said. "I must go. Don't tell Father I was here. It'll just upset him."

Jakie smiled. Samuel was so like his father.

"He misses you, son."

"He misses me, does he!" Samuel could hide his anger no longer. "When Father had to choose between his tradition and his son," he said tersely, "he chose against his son. So he can't miss me much." He spit the words across the dismal kitchen as though they were mad dogs turned loose after long years of prison. Samuel sighed. "Besides, what if I find Emily? He'll never accept her. He called her a pagan." There were tears in his eyes now. The wrath was gone out of him. "I must be heading back."

"I thought you said you were passing through, son," she said, a quiver in her throat. "You aren't, are you?" *You came to see us, didn't you?*

"Good-bye, Mother," he said, without looking back. And Samuel was gone as quickly as he had come.

"Good-bye, son. We'll always be waiting for

you to come home." She was crying now,
silently with head bowed, and Jakie went to
stir the fire so he didn't have to look at her.

The father says, "My son is wrong
To go his stubborn way."
The son replies, "I guess he's right
If growing up's my way."
But Mother's love has other ways.
"A son is never not a son," she says.
"Someday our family will be one."

The son retorts, "My dad's a fake,
No better he than me."
The father snorts, "Get out of here
And don't come back to me."
But Mother's love has other ways.
"A son is never not a son," she says.
"Someday our family will be one."

The father shouts, "I wish I had
A son as sons should be."
The son cries, "Dad, I want a Dad,
And you are none to me."
But Mother's love has other ways.
"A son is never not a son," she says.
"Someday our family will be one."

The village grew. Many sections developed, each with its own traditions. Then one day visitors from another kingdom invaded the village. They convinced some of the villagers to leave and travel to other villages in the name of God's love. Change came to the village. New houses were built, each unique in its own way.

"Let's go in," he said. "I'm tired of living outside."

"Thank God for visiting us," she said. "A new day has come."

They took down their tent and went in through the gate. Some of the villagers welcomed them and offered to help them build a house.

"We'll keep our tent," he said. "We'll pitch it on the edge of the village so we can leave if they try to burn us."

"Welcome to my people," she said. "I never thought you'd join us. God will take care of us."

Some of the newcomers to the village spoke strange tongues. Their houses didn't look like houses to some of the older villagers. And their customs confused their neighbors.

"Some of the people talk of the good old

days," she said.

"Diversity is a blessing," he said. "It takes more love. But it's the only way I could have become one of these."

She smiled at him. "Now you have a name, too."

He took her into the tent and they made love. They named their child, Son-of-These, even before he was born. And he grew up in the village, in his parents' tent, listening to the tales of the villagers and playing games with the children of other newcomers.

"We're happy at last," she said, and he kissed her as they watched their boy with his friends.

Our God creates us every day, forgives us every night, binds up our wounds, and comforts us as a mother soothes her child. He builds reunion, joy, and peace in all of us.

Reviving

The time:	*The place:*
MANY TIMES	**ALL OVER THE WORLD**

Brothers and sisters, we must repent, the preacher said. *The harvest is past.* We must come back to God. *Summer is ended, we are not saved.* Face-to-face, pleading, late in the night, singing long past, lingering in echoes. *Daughter of my people am I hurt.* We must accept the love of Jesus who died and rose again *I am black* that we might have new life *astonishment* new life *hath taketh hold on me*

"I've found new peace of heart and I thank God," the old woman said, her black skin shining in the heat of the mission.

The man from near Moody nodded, his white hand clenching the Bible over his head. "The traditions must go," he cried throughout the tent. "We need renewal that will help us find new ways

Is there no balm He hath borne in Gilead?

of doing things."

The boy on the cycle shrugged. "Some people get too emotional at these revival meetings."

"Amen!"

our griefs and carried our sorrows

"I've never experienced anything like it in my life," said a young woman, brushing Russia's latest snow from her coat. "My father came with tears in his eyes and asked forgiveness — fathers usually don't, you know — and we were reconciled. I never believed it could happen."

He roared the cycle. "Not that I have anything against revival."

The Arab shrugged. "Something must be wrong with me, because it didn't catch on —"

"I'll never be the same again," the old woman sighed.

smitten of God, and afflicted; wounded

We need a revival, the preacher said. And no one else can do it for us. We must come back to God ourselves *all we like sheep without one plea.* (What used to be important is now unimportant *I come* and what used to be insignificant has now become enormously significant) *His stripes we are healed*

"I felt led of God to speak to you, brother."

"Really?"

"God has touched my life and given me peace,

and I believe He could do the same for you."

"Thank you, sister. If God wants me, He knows where to find me."

wretch like me

Where goes this people?
  We follow God, our God, from where we've been to where we know not.
These people — do they follow blindly?
  We follow blindly, yes, if faith be blind. We be blind or sighted with our God, for deafness and hearing matters not to faith.
Who is this people's God?
  We cannot tell, we do not know. Our God has love much greater than His unknown name. Our God creates us every day, forgives us every night, binds up our wounds, and comforts us as a mother soothes her child. Our God stands within the whisper and dwells within the thunder, building an Eden for us between the immovable mountain and the changing sands, an Eden for us each and all, reunion, joy and peace.

He was in the world, and the world was made by Him, and the world knew Him not.

English:
  We have come to tell you that God loves you. We have come to bring you the good news that Jesus can save even uncivilized people.

Spanish:

(bewildered) I don't understand a word you say.

German:

We have come to tell you about salvation. God gave His Son Jesus and He died for your sins.

Spanish:

What do you want with my people?

English:

Won't you be saved?

German:

God loves you.

Spanish:

You are foreigners to my country and I see you carry no swords — so you are welcome. But I understand nothing that you say. Perhaps you should just not talk.

English:

It's too bad you speak a strange language. I'll teach you English.

German:

I'll teach you German.

Spanish:

(laughing and gesturing) You are welcome but you speak a strange language.

Is there no amazing physician there grace

Arabic:

Our revival brought me to believe that our church should not be a lot of people who look and act the same. It should be a fellowship of very different people who gather to

share a common faith and scatter to spread
the good news that God loves us.
God is calling us, the preacher said   *peace*
    to love all men   *gave he power*
      hath broken every barrier down
to bring out fears   and hatreds to Him
    joy   to be cleansed
      repent   *repent*

"My name is Egla Birmingham," the black
girl said.

The young man extended his hand. "I'm
Elias George from Jordan."

"I'm from Panama."

"I'm Alta Walter from Pennsylvania," the
white girl said. They shook hands.

"Are you enjoying this Mennonite World
Conference?"

"Yes, very much," Alta said. "I never realized
how many different kinds of Mennonites and
Mennonite Brethren and Amish and Brethren-
in-Christ there are all over the world."

Egla nodded. "It's amazing. The sense of
being different and yet at the same time
united is really marvelous."

"I agree," Elias joined in. "There were some
sad aspects to the revival movement, some
terrible imperialism and oppression. But there
also are some wonderful sides to revival too.
It has brought us together here at Curitiba."

"That's the fantastic thing about renewal,"
Alta said. "When God visits us, things can never
be the same again."

We need love, the preacher said. We must
repent.

The Lord knows us each,
Yet one we appear;
As dots form a line,
And sands fill a beach;
He's asking us here,
"Are these people Mine?"

As selves and as church
The Lord shaped us both
His people and mine;
Alone is the search,
Together the growth,
"Yes, Lord, we are Thine!"

And the boy grew. And his mother taught him the traditions of her people. "We are God's children," she said.

At first the boy accepted her words, and reveled in her stories of the fires, and the long journey, and the village as it used to be. He liked to hear her tell him how his father had adopted her people.

The boy played with his friends and sometimes told them his mother's stories. But his friends laughed at him. "Don't believe those old-fashioned legends," they said. "God's love isn't limited to the old village."

Sometimes Son-of-These traveled with his friends to other villages to tell them the truth. He saw many strange sights and met lots of interesting people. Once he met a girl from the big city, and he asked her all about it. They stayed up all night, talking and exchanging stories. He found her exciting, but her tales shocked him. He was glad to go home.

His mother and father knew of his trips, and cautioned him. "God's love is here among your people," they said. But the boy's friends convinced him to go with them. "The city needs us," they said. And so he went with them. He met the girl again, and she invited him to her house.

"We live in a tent," Son-of-These said, as he sat in her house.

"A tent? That's primitive," she said.

"It is? I didn't know." He liked the girl and felt embarrassed by his lack of knowledge. "My name is Son-of-These," he said. "What's yours?"

She laughed. "A tent and a name! How antiquated can you get?" The girl was bold and voluptuous, and the boy was a bit frightened.

"What is your name?" he asked.

"Names are out of date," she said, caressing him. "Love is all that matters."

"How do you know who you are?" he asked her. "How can you love someone who has no name?"

She kissed him. "If you want me enough," she said, "you'll give up your name."

He wanted her, so he asked her no more about names. She showed him the city, and he met many people, all without names. There were no families. The people in the city worked with machines, and knew nothing of the soil.

He missed the village, but he loved the girl.

So he tried to forget his parents' tent. He worked with machines, and made many things. And each day he attempted to love all the nameless people. But he found it difficult.

One day, after many years, he received a message that his mother was dying. "Come home, Son-of-These," his father wrote. But he would not have gone, if the girl had not insisted. "I want to see the village," she said. "I want to go with you."

They arrived in the winter, and found his mother near death. The soil was old, and the villagers were starving. But his parents kissed him, and fed him, and said his name over and over.

And the girl loved the village, poor as it was. "You are so lucky," she said. "Why did you leave? Let's stay here and find us a name."

"It's too late," he said. "The winter is here, and the village is dead."

94

Backward Nate Beiler

The time:
THE PRESENT

The place:
AMERICA

Nate Beiler was hoeing his garden. It was evening. On Amish farms, gardens are women's work in the daytime, but in the evening when the fieldwork is finished, the men help with the garden too. It's a way of cooling off with the day.

Nate pulled a weed, shook the soil from its roots, and threw it on the ground. He turned to his wife, Lucy, who was hoeing two rows away.

"I don't understand why Levi wants more schooling," he said. "Certainly there's enough to be learned here on the farm."

"I agree, Nathan. What you don't know can't hurt you."

Nate stood leaning on his hoe as he looked toward the house. The children were playing in the yard. That was good. Children should play a little now and then. They had worked so hard in the fields today.

He spit the way all good farmers spit. "I guess no one stopped around to look at the farm today, Lucy," he asked.

"Turn your back, Nathan. There's a woman down there along the road with a camera." Lucy was disgusted.

Lucy stopped hoeing for a minute. She worked hard. Too hard, he sometimes thought. Not many Amish women looked so pretty after so many children and so much work.

"No, they didn't, Nathan," she said, wiping her forehead. "Not a soul. Well, I should say no one except tourists out along the road. They are such a bother."

Nate sighed. "I'm sure there won't be any tourists pestering us in Guatemala."

"No tourists and no expensive farms. Our children will be able to grow up normal there."

They went back to hoeing. A black woman stopped her car out along the road and came up along the garden fence, camera in hand.

"Yes, I hope so," Nate was saying. "The world here in Lancaster is becoming so frantic. There's no peace and quiet anymore. You know, Lucy, maybe we should just sell to the Stoltzfus brothers."

Lucy saw the woman with the camera. "Turn your back, Nathan. There's a woman down there along the road with a camera."

Nate looked just in time to see the woman snap a photo. He turned away quickly.

"Seems like they never stop coming." Lucy was disgusted. "It makes it seem almost as though we're the abnormal ones, the way they snap photographs."

"Now, Lucy, don't get excited. You can't expect them to understand how foolish they are. They aren't farmers. They're ignorant of a lot of this stuff."

"It's a shame."

"I agree, Lucy. It is a shame the way these worldly people carry on." He spit again. Why did the tourists have to come, he had wondered so many times. And the women are always dressed so scantily, with no shame.

Suddenly he noticed the woman coming closer. "She's coming toward us, Lucy," he said, hoeing furiously. "You handle her."

The black woman had a deep voice. "Hi," she called over the fence, "I'm Rosa Johnson. May I take your picture?"

Lucy kept hoeing. "Please don't."

"Would you prefer if I did not?"

"Please don't."

"I'm sorry. I didn't mean to offend you. Don't you believe in cameras?"

"No, we don't." Lucy was doing pretty good.

"Really!" the black woman exclaimed, with a self-conscious laugh. "I didn't know that. What's wrong with a camera?"

Nate wondered what Lucy would say. It was all there in the Bible, but how do you explain that to such people?

"We believe in living life, not freezing it," Lucy was saying to the woman. "God's the Creator, you know."

Nate tried not to laugh. It was a good answer, but it almost made his wife sound educated. Not for long.

"*Vie dumm sindt sie?*" she asked Nate in the Pennsylvania Dutch dialect.

"*Schick sie doch weg,*" he answered, telling Lucy to send her away.

"I must work in my garden now," Lucy told
98

the woman.

"May I help? I've always wanted to live on an Amish farm," the woman said loudly, pronouncing the "A" in Amish so that it sounded like the "A" in Amos.

Nate was about to interrupt and tell this woman to clear out when he heard someone at the other end of the garden. He turned to see Norman Harnish pointing toward him.

"Oh, there you are," Norman shouted in his wheezy, high-pitched voice. "Nathan, I have a couple interested in seeing the farm. May I show them around?"

Nate glanced at Lucy apologetically. Then he walked toward Norman. "I should have told you not to come, Norman. I think it's sold."

But the real estate salesman had already motioned to a couple coming across the yard toward the garden. They must have come in the back way.

"Hey, come in here," Norman was calling so loud the neighbors could probably hear him in the quiet evening. "Let me show you around."

Nate could have died when he saw the couple. City people. The man dressed fancy and wore a moustache. He was puffing on a cigarette. And the woman — Nate looked away. She was wearing a dress so short and so tight and low cut that she looked naked. Worldly naked.

"Don't let me interrupt anything. Nathan," Norman was saying. "I know a garden needs a lot of work." Then he shifted his voice into a sort of salesman yelp. "Now, Mr. and Mrs.

Manazak, this here farm belongs to Nathan
Beiler. That's him there with the hoe. He said
I could show you around a little."

Whereupon the pretty man walked right into
the garden and came down the row with hand
outstretched. "Hello, Mr. Beiler. I'm Teddy
Manazak." Nate nodded, but didn't shake hands.
The man looked at Lucy. "Mrs. Beiler, my plea-
sure, he said with a flourish. He gestured.
"That's my wife, Gwen."

The naked woman had a harsh voice.
"Theodore, don't bother the poor souls," she
rasped. "Get out of their garden." She lit a
cigarette and puffed vigorously.

Manazak noticed Rosa by the fence. "I take
it you work here," he blurted.

Nate was surprised by his comment.

"No, I'm a teacher," the black woman answered indignantly. "I'm studying the Amish."

"Aren't we all?" Gwen snapped.

Norman was still bubbling with sales talk.
"This would make a wonderful country estate,
Mr. Manazak."

Country estate! Nate was horrified. Farms are
for farming, not city-folk estates.

Manazak smiled broadly, rubbing his hands
together. "We must make room for progress!"

"Where are you from?" the black woman
asked.

"New Jersey."

"I'm from California."

Gwen strutted a step toward the teacher.
"Taking your turn at slumming?"

"This isn't a slum, honey," Rosa shot back.

100

"This is a zoo."

"Not after we buy it, darling. Our security guards understand privacy and they keep it that way for us."

Nate wondered what they meant.

"Now this barn here is one of the finest structures around," Norman was saying. "Built in 1824, it's still in excellent shape. The house was built two years later and has twelve rooms, an attic and a cellar."

Gwen interrupted. "Does the place have a springhouse? I've always dreamed of having my own springhouse. I read about them one time in a book long ago."

Norman nodded. "Yes, this farm has a springhouse and a smokehouse."

Manazak smiled broadly again. "Good. A place to smoke."

"Meats."

"What?"

"Meats."

"A place for smoking meats, Theodore."

"Oh, meats."

"Yeah, meats."

Rosa turned to Nate. "Mr. Beiler, why are you selling your farm to these people who don't know what a farm is?"

"I haven't sold it yet."

Manazak rushed down the row so fast that Lucy looked at Nate with a bewildered question in her face. "We'll outbid any offer you've had," he said loudly between puffs.

"Don't be careless, Teddy," the naked woman warned. "We want some money left over to fix up the place a little. It's so depressingly simple."

Nate was getting a little bewildered himself. "We like things simple," he said without looking at her.

Rosa persisted. "Why are you selling, Mr. Beiler?"

Norman answered with authority in his tone. "They're moving to Guatemala."

"In Central America?"

"Wherever Guatemala is. Now, Mr. Manazak, there's ten acres of woodland that go with this farm. And of course the creek — "

"Let's talk money," Gwen demanded.

"I was going to explain about the land."

"I don't care about the land. I want to talk money."

Lucy moved over beside Nate. "Be careful, Nathan. These people aren't farmers."

"Why do Amish move to Guatemala?" Rosa asked.

Norman corrected her pronunciation while Gwen responded with a tone of condescension. "I guess they want to get away from the modern world. I read someplace they don't like technology."

"What do you know about it?" the black woman laughed. "Maybe they're smarter than the rest of us. While we got wrapped up in test tubes and statistics and progress, these people developed a way of life, complete with answers to the most difficult questions."

Norman grunted. "I thought we were selling a farm."

"Norman, I think maybe I better sell it to the Stoltzfus brothers. They gave me a good offer."

"How much, Mr. Beiler?" Manazak pushed in. "How much? I'll do better."

"You will?"

"Careful, Nathan. Remember why we're moving." Lucy was concerned.

Nate looked at Lucy, then back to Manazak. Why don't these people go away, he thought. He knew he'd never sell it to them. They didn't know the first thing about soil.

"Nathan," wheezed Norman, "I think you should at least listen to their offer."

"Mr. Beiler, I'll give you twenty percent more than your highest offer." Manazak smiled broadly as though he had just surprised everybody.

Nate puckered his mouth. Then he smiled for the first time. His mind was made up. "I'll let you know," he said to the city slicker who continued blowing smoke in his face.

Manazak was stunned. "Let us know! You gotta sell! I'm offering you the money."

"Money's not everything." Nate looked at Lucy and her eyes approved. Get them out of here, she seemed to say.

The naked lady was not to be undone. "Theodore, I want this farm," she snorted, her voice harsh and unpleasant.

Norman knew Nate wouldn't sell. "They often sell to their own people, you know," he said quietly in his now normal voice, the sales pitch gone as he tried to explain it to the three visitors who stood in the Beilers' garden.

"Even for less money?"

Nate smiled at his wife. They were happy again. "We must help each other," he said. "The world is creeping in around us and we are forgetting the ways of peace."

The Manazaks had already gone. Norman lingered to peer at the gable end of the old farmhouse, as though studying its worth. The black schoolteacher was putting her camera in her big handbag. "Why is it that backward sometimes seems so forward?" she asked herself aloud as she walked away.

Lucy watched them go and breathed deeply, "The world wants peace too," she said, her voice sad. "But they're not willing."

Nate nodded and they went back to hoeing. The children were playing in the yard, the evening was cool and quiet, and Guatemala wasn't far away.

Nate Beiler was a backward man,
Or so I've heard it said,
But why's he know the answer to
The questions on ahead?

> *If he's so dumb*
> *Pray tell how come*
> *Poor backward Nate*
> *Seems up-to-date*
> *Comparing to with from.*

If Nate's as backward as they say
With honest simple guide,
Why's modern man appear confused
With progress on his side?

> *If he's so dumb*
> *Pray tell how come*
> *Poor backward Nate*
> *Seems up-to-date*
> *Comparing to with from.*

Nate Beiler's modern as they come
If modern's full of life,
For backward races on ahead
When backward's loving life.

> *If he's so dumb*
> *Pray tell how come*
> *Poor backward Nate*
> *Seems up-to-date*
> *Comparing to with from.*

One-of-These was glad to see her son, and
got well. But many of the villagers were dying.
Their children had left long ago, for other
villages. Some even went to the city.

Strangers moved into the village and watched
the old people die. They buried the old-timers
outside the village, near the east gate. They
burned their houses and split up the land.

"Come to the city with us," the girl said to
his parents. "We can build a village there."

"But I don't want a village," replied Son-of-
These. "Love is all that matters."

"How can you love people unless you know
who they are?" the girl asked.

"You sound like my parents."

"Perhaps. Probably more like my own parents."

"I thought you had no name."

"I lied. I had a name, and a people. But I
left them to find love."

His parents decided to stay behind. "God led
us here," they said. "You go where He leads
you. And don't forget to give thanks."

And so Son-of-These and the girl returned.
They went about building a village in the city.
"We'll be known as the people of love," they

said. "Let all who love the name of our God join in our community." And they were happy.

But many who believed in love and came to the village had different customs. They battled much as each sought to control the life of the village. And soon there were fires. Some moved out to form their own villages.

The girl was angry. "We were supposed to be God's people," she stormed.

Son-of-These tried to comfort her. "Villages are funny places, my love. Outside the village, we are lost. Inside, we are hurt. That's how it was in my parents' village, too."

"Then why doesn't God do something about it?" she asked.

He kissed her. "He does. Moment by moment. That's where the faith comes in."

They sat overlooking the village in the midst of the city. They wept for a bit. And then they gave thanks.

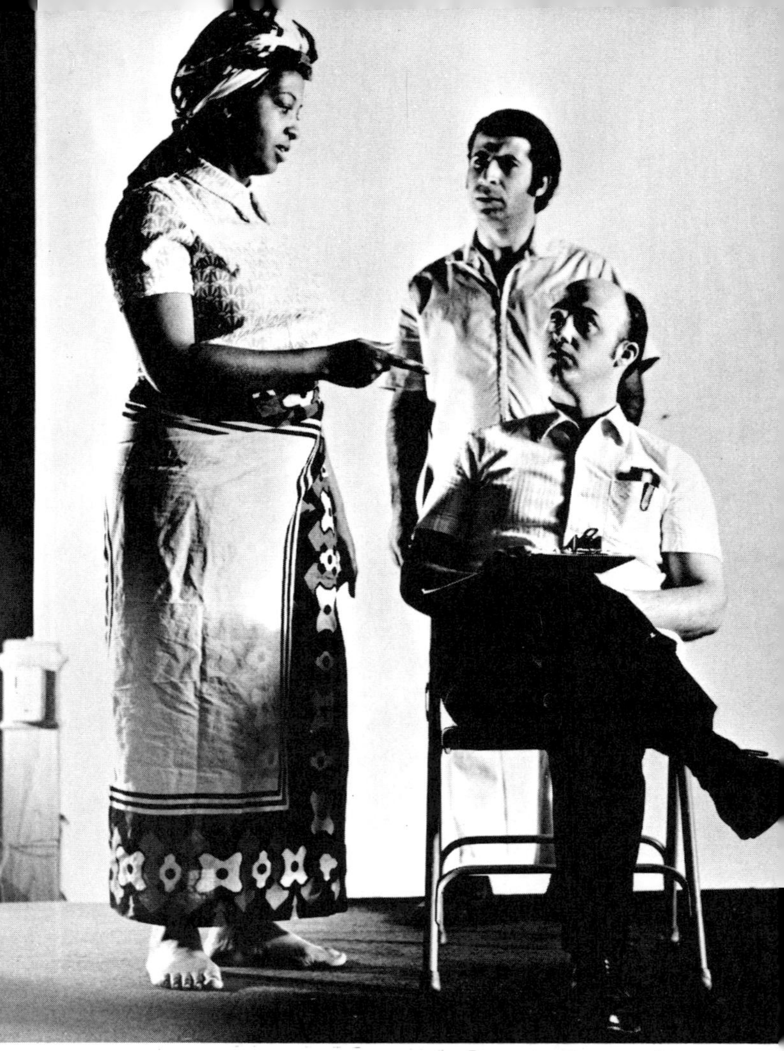

"You've no right assuming that you're the administrator around here," I told him. "This is not your country. You're welcome here, but you're no longer in control."

Trust Is a Two-Way Street

The time:
THE PRESENT

The place:
AFRICA

Dear God,

I wish You had been there. Abram was sitting at his desk like an indifferent American. And I came in and looked at him, working with the figures. Now there's something that always makes me mad — the way these foreigners presume to know how to spend our money. I shouldn't call it "our" money, except that it is just that. Well, ours and Yours. But not Abram's. He's just a missionary.

Anyhow, Abram gives me the eye, and I know he's thinking, "What's that African girl doing in here again?" I've been bugging him a lot since I got back from the States, and it's no wonder he gets irritated. But I want to irritate him. Missionaries need to be pushed around now and then or they'll just think it's their place. (Which it ain't.)

"You've no right assuming that you're the administrator around here," I told him. "This is not your country. You're welcome here, but you're no longer in control."

Wow, that got him going. "Mary," he says,

using the name the missionaries had given me
as a child. "Mary, take it easy. Let's talk a
little sense. If we're going to keep this hospital
running the way it should, we need funds. And
I'm the man to get the funds."

"Why?" says I.

"What?" says he.

I laughed. We were speaking in English and I
think it makes Abram a little uptight to see
me using his language in my country with as
much facility as he does. Sometimes I think I
understand English better than he does. (Sorry
if that sounds boastful.)

"When the missionaries came here thirty
years ago," I says to Abram, "we were glad to
see you. You helped us learn to read, you
taught us medicine, you gave us Christian
names, and you shared the good news of God's
love. Thanks a lot."

He wasn't listening. So I talked louder.

"You brought a million other things with you
too, things that were enslaving and wrong. But
let me tell you, Abram, the missionary input
is beginning to fall out."

"Do I have to listen to this again?"

"Don't patronize me, Abram."

"I wasn't."

"You most certainly were. You missionaries
brought a set of cultural values that I find
repulsive, if you want to know what I think."

"As though I didn't know."

"You really think you can mouth me any way
you wish, don't you? Well, times have changed,
Abram. One of these days we'll send you back

110

to your father's farm in good old America, and then we won't have to listen to your demands any more.''

''You're the demanding one.''

To say that Abram makes me furious would be an understatement. He's about forty-five, getting a little bald and a bit gray. And he acts like he owns the world. All in Your name, of course.

I was ready to storm out, but Mohammed walked in.

''When are we going to improve things around here?'' he asked Abram. Mohammed's a doctor whom Abram brought down from one of those Arab countries about two years ago, while I was in the States. But You know that.

Anyhow, I feel Mohammed just plays into Abram's hand. So I says, ''You're asking the wrong man, doctor.''

''Sorry,'' says he, ''are you the right man, Mary?''

Of course both of them laughed. But let them, I don't care. They think women like me don't understand what church is all about, but that's where they're wrong.

''Remember, Mohammed,'' I told him, ''you're a foreigner here too. The local church must make these decisions, and we have not yet made up our minds.''

''But Abram's the mission administrator. You gotta accept some structures, Mary.''

''Let him administrate the mission then. We'll manage the church.'' Abram was finally listening to me.

"What does that mean?" he asked. "What's the difference between mission and church, Mary?"

"Church is us. Mission is you."

Mohammed got a little red in the face. "Don't give me any of that we-you stuff, Mary. Of course, we're of different nationalities. But we're trying to work together here. That's the whole reason they asked me to come to this hospital."

Abram nodded. "You're an excellent doctor, too."

"Thank you, Abram. What I mean, Mary, is that we Mennonites believe that the miracle of God's love is demonstrated in how people of different cultures can work together. Like us."

I couldn't help laughing. "That's ridiculous."

Abram stood up and came over to me. "Mary, you understand what he means, don't you?"

That's the trouble with missionaries. Always insulting a person's intelligence. "Of course I understand what the doctor's trying to say. But with his background, he should be the first to see the error in his hope."

"Hope?"

"Mennonites have a lot to learn about inter-cultural relationships."

Abram came right back. "You're using 'they' again," he said. I must say he surprised me. I didn't think he was that smart.

"Maybe I don't consider myself an automatic Mennonite, Abram. I've been to your college in the States. I know how you understand your-selves."

Mohammed snapped his fingers. "How's all this going to help the hospital?"

"You use the word 'help' too much, Mohammed. The time for help is passing. To foreigners, help means control."

I was sorta proud of myself. I was holding my own against two foreigners, two men, and my English was flawless. I wish You had been there.

"I'm not ignorant of that, Mary," the doctor said.

Abram was beginning to recover. "You know your people hold all the leadership positions in the church here," he said.

"Then just back off."

"What?"

"Let us make the decisions, Abram. If we are indeed the church, let us have complete control."

"But there's a lot of money involved."

"Same old dollar trick!"

"What?"

I was sure he understood what I meant. "Abram, it's money expenditures that decide who's in charge. You know that much."

"Of course I do."

Mohammed interrupted. "I guess, Mary, I feel I owe a lot to the missionaries who came to my country."

Abram, meanwhile, was staring at me as though I had hit him on the head. "What am I to do?" he asked. "What's my function, Mary?"

"That's exactly what I'd like to know."

Mohammed tried to salvage the argument

with some clear, emphatic Arab reasoning.
"Mary, none of your people have the fiscal
experience that Abram has. And our hospital
must be run efficiently in order to keep it going."

Abram walked over and looked me in the eye
for the first time. "Mary," he said firmly, "the
question is whether you trust us."

"Trust is a two-way street," Mohammed
chimed in.

But I didn't give an inch. "You're wrong,"
I said. "The question is whether you trust
us."

That's when You interrupted. I wonder how
long You were there. "We need another
Schleitheim," You said. And we all just looked
at each other and said, "What does that mean?"

I thought I'd ask You myself. Or maybe it's
a secret.

Love,

Mary

It isn't walls of glass and steel
That keep us fenced apart,
Nor do our differences reveal
That only years, miles, tongues can steal
Forgiveness heart from heart.

It's who we are that builds that wall,
Creation wars the cross;
Each battles unity of all,
Yet He who shaped both great and small
Will bridge love's peace across.

*Once again, his mother was near death.
They traveled to the old village and found his
parents sequestered in the back part of a
shabby building where the poor lived.*

*One-of-These was at peace. She watched her
son greet his father with tears of joy. The girl
was more beautiful than she had remembered
as she stood by the door, her little ones hiding
in her skirts.*

*"Come to me, my children," One-of-These
called. "We must give thanks for each other. We
must thank God in life and in death."*

*They stood around her bed, warmed by her
joy, touched by her faith. They sang a hymn of
love, and shared the sacred stories of the fire,
the journey, and the village as it used to be.*

*"Most of my people are at the Great
Reunion," she said. "But I'm in no rush, because I got reunion here."*

*Son-of-These went to his father. "Are you
glad you adopted her people?" he asked.*

"I should have sooner," he replied.

*The girl lifted her children onto the bed. They
all put their arms around each other and made
love, oblivious to the strangers watching from the
tower nearby.*

116

"We're like a people all by ourselves," one of
the children said.

The girl kissed the child as Son-of-These
held her in his arms. "This is heaven," he
said. "I'm so glad we're here."

And then One-of-These began to sing.

Are these people mine? The question is God's, but also it's ours. Who wants them? Who needs them?

Reunion Time

The time:	*The place:*
THE FUTURE	**GOD KNOWS**

(Spot down as lights come up on reunion scene. Actors enter dressed as characters they played in earlier scenes. Scene begins with Mary alone on the stage. Hans enters.)

Hans:

I think God has saved us. I believed He would. I'm not sure I know you, friend.

Mary:

My Christian name is Mary. I'm thinking of changing it to my old name.

Hans:

Were you at Schleitheim?

Mary:

Why's everyone talking about Schleitheim?

Elfrieda:

(entering) I'm from Chortitza, and Cornelius and I are on the way to the promised land.

Hans:

Welcome. (they shake hands)

Mary:

Nice to have you. (they shake) Where's the promised land?

Anneken:

(entering with Dirk) The promised land is
where we all gather together in the presence
of our Lord and Savior.

Dirk:

Death cannot be the enemy if love goes on
before.

Elfrieda:

Cornelius always says the harvest is ahead
of us, not behind.

Mohammed:

(entering) I was scared I'd miss the reunion.
How do you do, brother? (shakes hands with
Hans) I'm Mohammed.

Hans:

I'm Hans. I used to live near the border.
Were you at Schleitheim?

Mohammed:

No, I wasn't. I was at Curitiba, though.

Hans:

Was that something like Schleitheim? Was
Brother Michael there? (turning) Why hello,
sister.

Lucy:

(entering) Hello. Which way to Guatemala?

Elfrieda:

Is that the promised land? I'll go along.

Mary:

Everyone's going on — seeking the future —
crossing the Red Sea. Is there no haven in
the earth for this people?

Samuel:

(entering) Not when you're seeking forgiveness
and can't find it. Has anyone seen Emily?

120

Mohammed:
Reunion time is here — but never quite complete. The cloud of heaven races on before us and we follow like a people seeking rest. (They all sing a hymn a cappella in slanted cross lighting and shadows. Then they sing the reunion finale, under full lights, portraying the people at work, the trials of persecution and drudgery of being refugees, the forgiveness of enemies, the family reunion, and finally the great reunion circle of praise. Lights down as finale concludes.)

Sweet reunion, we are one,
Praise the Lord, thanksgiving bring;
Take my hand, O promised land,
God's reunion, shout and sing!

Epilogue

Are these people mine?

The question is God's, but also it's ours.

A movement that flamed in those dark days of Reformation, centuries ago, when the world was being broken up again, thank God, and faith was being compromised by Rome and Wittenberg alike, God forbid, men and women of faith, soon without leaders, were caught in a chaotic swirl of radical love and a restitution of the faith of Peter, James, and John.

A movement flaming in a thousand different hearts, pursued and persecuted, fleeing to the hills and caves and countryside, tried to cope with all the dying — and friends, a lot of us are here today because our forefathers held their tongues.

The movement settled down before the second generation took the reins. The movement became a people, a remnant — or was it a residue? And centuries passed in withdrawn silence as the people tried to cope with living. The dying never stopped, but the living was the harder for the quiet in the land.

Are these people mine? Who wants them

— these backward German farmers? Who wants them? Who needs them?

The sameness was the people's refuge, not the flame of movement. And sameness filled the years with ways of doing things. Tradition captured the remnant, chased from country to country, killed for refusing to kill.

And not long ago, God brought revival to this people, thrusting them back into the marketplace in Russia, America, and Africa.

Now the sameness is breaking up, the flame is burning up the tradition, and the residue is seeking for the gold among the dross. Sometimes it looks like a lot of dross, sometimes like a great culture of a pilgrim people.

And the flame of the movement that started everything erupts with another chaotic swirl of radical love and a restitution of the faith of Peter, James, and John — and Conrad, Michael, and Menno too.

The Author

Born the fourth of seven sons, Merle Good grew up a Mennonite farm boy in Lancaster County, Pennsylvania.

He and his wife, Phyllis, now live and teach at Lancaster Mennonite High School, from which he graduated in 1964. They also serve as producers of the Dutch Family Festival in Lancaster each summer. Good's special interest is storytelling and the dramatic arts.

Good received his BA from Eastern Mennonite College, Harrisonburg, Virginia, and completed his MDiv degree at Union Theological Seminary, New York City, in 1972.

He has authored one previous book, a novel, *Happy as the Grass Was Green*, which has been filmed as a major motion picture starring Geraldine Page and Pat Hingle.

126